DRAGONS

by
Charis Mather

Minneapolis, Minnesota

Credits
All images are courtesy of Shutterstock.com, unless otherwise specified. With thanks to Getty Images, Thinkstock Photo, and iStockphoto.

Recurring images – Yauhen Paleski, Dedraw Studio, SpicyTruffel, Gaidamashchuk. 4–5 – Liu Zishan, tomertu, Macrovector. 6–7 – Vac1. 8–9 – Josep.Ng, Panaiotidi, T Studio, Willyam Bradberry, MR1805. 10–11 – adike, Melkor3D. 12–13 – Dotted Yeti, eddystocker, Bibadash, GoodStudio, Leena Robinson. 14–15 – Dark Geometry, iWUTJRW. 16–17 – Melkor3D, Storozhenko, Susanitah, Imogen/Adobe Stock. 18–19 – Daniel Eskridge, Digital Storm. 20–21 – NeagoneFo, Robert Keresztes, Sergey Uryadnikov. 22–23 – patpitchaya, talitha_it.

Bearport Publishing Company Product Development Team
President: Jen Jenson; Director of Product Development: Spencer Brinker; Managing Editor: Allison Juda; Associate Editor: Naomi Reich; Associate Editor: Tiana Tran; Senior Designer: Colin O'Dea; Associate Designer: Elena Klinkner; Associate Designer: Kayla Eggert; Product Development Assistant: Owen Hamlin

Library of Congress Cataloging-in-Publication Data

Names: Mather, Charis, 1999- author.
Title: Dragons / by Charis Mather.
Description: Fusion books. | Minneapolis, Minnesota : Bearport Publishing
  Company, [2024] | Series: Mythical creatures | "This edition is
  published by arrangement with BookLife Publishing"--T.p. verso.
Identifiers: LCCN 2023031017 (print) | LCCN 2023031018 (ebook) | ISBN
  9798889163022 (library binding) | ISBN 9798889163077 (paperback) | ISBN
  9798889163114 (ebook)
Subjects: LCSH: Dragons--Juvenile literature.
Classification: LCC GR830.D7 M375 2024 (print) | LCC GR830.D7 (ebook) |
  DDC 398.24/54--dc23/eng/20230712
LC record available at https://lccn.loc.gov/2023031017
LC ebook record available at https://lccn.loc.gov/2023031018

© 2024 BookLife Publishing
This edition is published by arrangement with BookLife Publishing.

North American adaptations © 2024 Bearport Publishing Company. All rights reserved. No part of this publication may be reproduced in whole or in part, stored in any retrieval system, or transmitted in any form or by any means, electronic, mechanical, photocopying, recording, or otherwise, without written permission from the publisher.

For more information, write to Bearport Publishing, 5357 Penn Avenue South, Minneapolis, MN 55419.

CONTENTS

Myths, Magic, and More **4**
What Does a Dragon Look Like? **6**
A Flying Beast **8**
Fire Breather **10**
This and That **12**
Different Dragons **14**
Where Dragons Live **16**
Mythical Look-Alikes **18**
Real-Life Dragons? **20**
Mysterious Mythical Creatures **22**
Glossary **24**
Index **24**

MYTHS, MAGIC, AND MORE

Most people have heard of the huge, magical beasts known as dragons. But you probably haven't seen one in real life. Why not? Because dragons are **mythical** creatures!

For thousands of years, people from all around the world have told stories about dragons. Different **legends** talk about the creatures in different ways. Let's learn what the stories have to say!

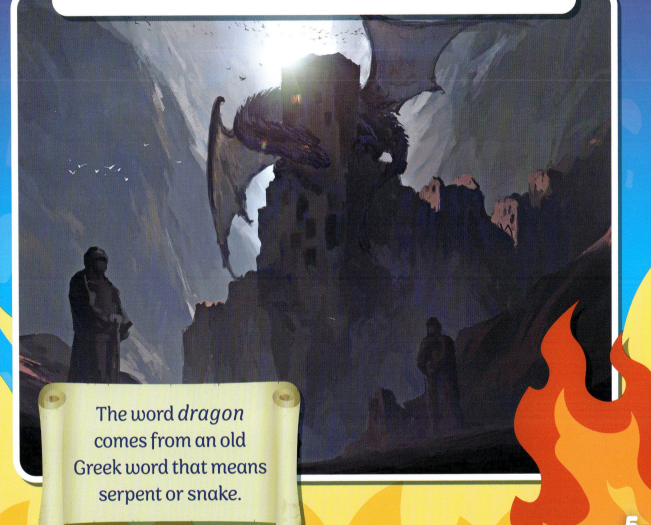

The word *dragon* comes from an old Greek word that means serpent or snake.

WHAT DOES A DRAGON LOOK LIKE?

Let's take a closer look at these big beasts.

Wings

Dragon wings don't have feathers. Instead, they are smooth like bat wings.

Tail

A long, **flexible** tail is thought to help a dragon fight.

A FLYING BEAST

One of the most amazing things about dragons is that they can fly! But could creatures so large even get off the ground?

Stories say that dragon wings were huge. Could wings much larger than the size of their bodies push lots of air to keep the beasts up in the sky?

Most animals have thick bones. But bird bones are mostly **hollow**. This makes them lighter. If dragons were real, maybe hollow bones would help them fly.

A bird's bone

Huge flying **reptiles** lived at the same time as dinosaurs. Some were as large as a small airplane!

FIRE BREATHER

Apart from fantastic flight, what else have we heard about these mythical creatures? Dragons can breathe fire!

All fires need three basic things. They need something to start the flame, such as a spark. They also need a **fuel** to keep them burning. Finally, fires need air.

Could an animal really make fire? Some people wonder if it could be possible. So far, nobody has found the answer.

THIS AND THAT

Stories say dragons can live for hundreds of years. That's a long time, but it isn't unheard of. Some Greenland sharks may be 500 years old!

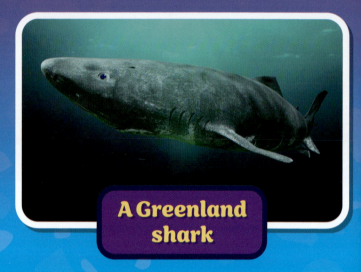

A Greenland shark

Legends say dragons hatch from small eggs. Many animals are born out of eggs!

Dragons are thought to be very **intelligent** creatures. Some stories say they're even smarter than people!

Scientists are finding out that lizards can be very smart.

DIFFERENT DRAGONS

Not all dragon tales are about wings and fire. Some of the first stories about dragons told of very different creatures that flew using magic powers.

These kinds of dragons were long and thin. They looked like giant snakes with legs. Many of their body parts seem to come from other animals.

An eagle's claw

A lion's mane

In many places, dragons are a sign of good luck.

WHERE DRAGONS LIVE

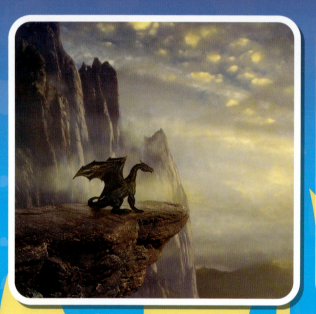

In many legends, dragons live far away from people. Dragons are said to make **lairs** in large mountain caves. Some stories tell of dragons using empty castles as their homes.

Piles of gold may be stored inside a dragon's lair. In stories, these beasts spend their lives collecting the shiny stuff. Then, they keep it close.

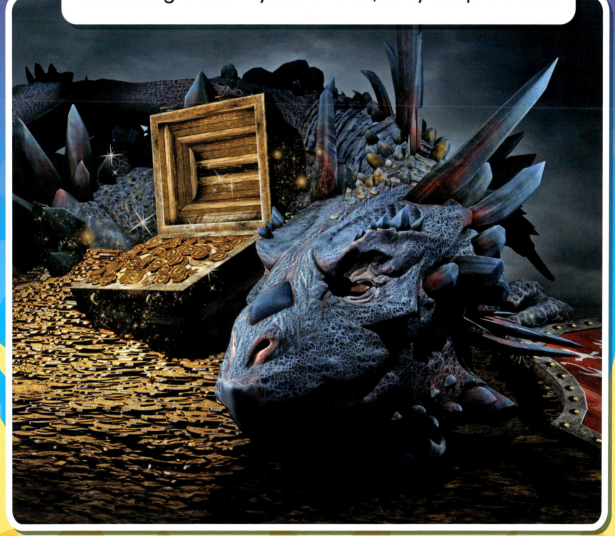

MYTHICAL LOOK-ALIKES

There are other mythical creatures like dragons. Let's take a look at a few.

A hydra

Hydras come from Greek myths. They are large, snakelike beasts with many heads. When one of these heads is cut off, more heads grow in its place!

Wyverns (WYE-vurnz) are mythical animals very similar to dragons. While dragons are usually thought to have four legs, wyverns are said to only have two.

A wyvern

Wyverns were sometimes put on flags to show strength.

REAL-LIFE DRAGONS?

Where do the stories of dragons come from? Maybe from real animals. . . .

Bearded Dragons

These calm lizards come from the deserts in Australia. Many people keep bearded dragons as pets.

Komodo Dragons

Komodo dragons are the world's largest lizards. They can be more than 10 feet (3 m) long. Sharp teeth help them catch animals to eat.

Draco Lizards

Also known as flying lizards, Draco lizards look almost like they take flight. Flaps of skin along the sides of their bodies help them **glide** from tree to tree.

MYSTERIOUS MYTHICAL CREATURES

Dragons are fun, mysterious creatures. We can learn a lot from stories about these big beasts.

If you can't get enough of dragons, just read some books! There is so much to explore about these magical, mythical creatures.

Some think stories of dragons started when people first found dinosaur bones!

GLOSSARY

flexible able to bend easily

fuel something that keeps a fire burning

glide to move in the air smoothly without flapping

hollow empty on the inside

intelligent very smart

lairs places where wild creatures live or rest

legends stories from the past that may have a mix of truth and made-up things

mythical based on stories or something made up in the imagination

reptiles cold-blooded animals that have dry, scaly skin and use lungs to breathe

scales small, hard skin parts found on animals such as fish and snakes

INDEX

bones 9, 23
eggs 12
fire 10–11, 14
hydras 18
lairs 16–17
legs 15, 19

lizards 13, 20–21
snakes 5, 15, 18
tails 6
teeth 7, 21
wings 6, 8, 14
wyverns 19